ALL THE BEST SKETCHES

LILLENAS® DRAMA

ALL
THE
BEST
SKETCHES

New Sketches from Best-Selling Authors
Martha Bolton, Jim Custer & Bob Hoose,
Chuck Neighbors, and Jeff Smith

Lillenas PUBLISHING COMPANY
KANSAS CITY, MO 64141

Questions? Please write or call:
    Lillenas Publishing Company
    Drama Resources
    P.O. Box 419527
    Kansas City, MO 64141
    Phone: 816-931-1900 • Fax: 816-412-8390
    E-mail: drama@lillenas.com
    Web site: www.lillenasdrama.com

Cover art by Kevin Williamson

Contents

The Gifts of the Spirit

by Jim Custer and Bob Hoose

Scripture References: 1 Corinthians 12:4-12; 1 Peter 4:8-11

Themes: Spiritual Gifts and Spiritual Growth

Cast:
GINNY—Perky, a bit ditzy, very helpful
TOM—Leader of the "Living Life to the Fullest" study. Tries to be in control, but definitely has his hands full
TED—Fairly straight kind of guy, has a good sense of humor
MERYDITH—Very organized, a tax consultant
CINDA—Sweet, caring kind of individual
RALPH—Somewhat moody because he's a little concerned about his gift

Setting: Simple with chairs in a semicircle

Props:
Cups
Paper and pen
Bible
Tape recorder

Lighting: Basic wash with a quick blackout

Running Time: 10 minutes

(Opens with people milling around)

GINNY: Coffee, anyone? Coffee.

RALPH: Here. Here. (GINNY *pours him coffee.)* Thanks.

TOM *(rushing in):* Sorry, I'm late. Traffic.

TED: It's OK, most of us just got here.

TOM: OK. Let's gather 'round and we'll get started.

MERYDITH: I made a list of everyone's names and phone numbers.

TOM: Very organized. Thank you, Merydith . . . that's great. OK, everyone . . . welcome, again, to "Living Life to the Fullest," a study in spiritual gifts. As I . . . .

MERYDITH: Excuse me . . . excuse me . . . just a little fast . . . Fullest . . . a study in spir-it . . . u-al gifts.

TOM: As I said last time, this eight-week study will, hopefully, help define for each one of us what our spiritual gifts are and how we can use them effectively. It's not . . .

MERYDITH (*writing, making a stopping noise*): . . . define for each one of us . . . what our spir-it-u-al . . .

TOM: Merydith. Merydith. You really don't have to take every word down. I'm not that interesting.

MERYDITH: I just don't want to miss anything.

TOM: You won't. We're just going to talk . . .

MERYDITH (*pulls out tape recorder and holds up microphone*): OK.

TOM: What kind of Christians make a difference in this world? (*All raise hands.*) It was just a rhetorical question.

(*All put hands down except* GINNY. *She notices and slowly puts hand down.* CINDA *enters in a rush.*)

CINDA: Sorry. I got detained. My next door neighbor wanted to talk about Christ . . . I've been praying for that . . . and today she just called on the phone and asked me to come over.

TOM: That's great. We were just getting started.

GINNY (*getting up*): Coffee?

CINDA: No thanks.

TOM: Now where was I?

MERYDITH: Uh . . . (*Reading*) What kind of Christians make a difference in this world?

TOM: Thank you. What kind of Christians make a difference in this world? (GINNY *starts to raise hand then quickly puts it down.*) Not talented ones, but healthy ones. And to be healthy we need to find out how we can be happy. To be happy we need to know how we can make a difference.

TED: That's where spiritual gifts come in?

TOM: Right. The spiritual gifts we're given, if used, can make a supernatural difference.

(*All excited.*)

RALPH: Supernatural?

GINNY: Sorta like Superman.

TOM: Not quite like that. You see, these are attributes that we are all supposed to use, but if we have been gifted in one of them, well, when we exercise it . . . it makes a supernatural difference.

GINNY: Like Wonder Woman!

TOM: Right, Ginny. Now, last week I gave you a list of gifts we find in 1 Corinthians and other places in scripture with their definitions. In looking them over, what do you think might be one of your spiritual gifts? Merydith?

MERYDITH: Well, I did sort of a spreadsheet of these on my computer . . . you know, listing the gifts, definitions, my likes and dislikes, possibilities, specific incidences of possible indications, correlating them together with high probability, and I've come up with . . . zero.

TOM: Pardon me?

MERYDITH: Not a clue. My computer went into overload and shut down. But I think maybe prophecy or one of the other top ones. Now, if I take prophecy . . . I don't have to wear something dusty or sack-ish, do I?

TOM: No.

MERYDITH: Good. Large, droopy clothing is a business no-no. When you're talking to a client they don't want to see a female Charlton Heston sitting on the other side of the desk.

TOM: I see. Ted?

TED: Uh . . . I just read them over . . . and I'm not sure either. My wife says I have the gift of channel changing.

MERYDITH: My husband too.

GINNY: Ooo . . . Mine too.

CINDA: Ditto.

GINNY: Must be a man's gift.

TED: But what I was thinking was . . . maybe wisdom . . . I guess that's why I'm here to find out.

TOM: Ginny.

GINNY: Well, I have two fruits.

TOM: Fruits?

GINNY: Of the spirit. I have two. Uh . . . discerning of spirits, and knowledge . . . I think. Just not sure which fruit I want. They're sorta like apples and oranges. (Laughs)

MERYDITH: They're gifts.

GINNY: I know, and I appreciate them, but one fruit is enough. Don't want to be greedy.

TOM: Ginny. I think there is a little bit of a misunderstanding. I think you're getting the phrase Gifts of the Spirit mixed up with the Fruit of the Spirit.

GINNY: Oh. Well, I like fruit better.

TOM: But it's a gift, not a fruit.

GINNY: I've given fruit before.

TOM: Never mind. Ralph?

RALPH: Uh . . . my gift, huh? Do I have to?

TOM: You don't want to?

RALPH: Well . . . *(with painful deliberation and much hesitation)* celibacy.

(Everyone except TOM looks a little shocked and says, "ooo.")

GINNY: What's that?

TOM *(ignoring GINNY)*: Why do you think so, Ralph?

RALPH: Well, I can't even get a date, so I figured I have to have it. I don't think I'm ever going to get married.

CINDA: Bless your heart.

RALPH: But I've decided that I don't want it. I'm going to give it back, and I'm going to take knowledge.

TED: Yeah, that way you'll know why you don't have a date.

(All laugh.)

RALPH: Funny. I know I probably have it 'cause I was the Trivial Pursuit champion at our last family reunion. Killed 'em.

TOM: Cinda?

CINDA: Well . . . evangelism, maybe faith. Understand . . . I don't go out and preach on the street corner or anything, and I'm no Billy Graham . . . I just, well, I seem to make a difference when I talk about Christ. People listen.

TOM: That's great . . . and that's what happens when we use our spiritual gifts.

MERYDITH: Now that we're talking about it . . . I think I'd like to trade. I'll trade you a prophecy for knowledge.

RALPH: I don't know. What else you got?

MERYDITH: I'll throw in one free tax consultation.

GINNY: Wait! Wait! As long as we're trading . . . I would like, uh, wisdom. *(To TED)* Can I have your wisdom? I'll give you discerning of spirits. I don't think it would come in handy . . . I don't drink.

(Everyone starts trading and talking.)

TOM: People . . . people. *(All quiet down.)* I see we have some work to do. Now let's turn to 1 Corinthians.

GINNY: Is that before or after Psalms?

TOM: After.

GINNY: Old or New Testament?

TOM: New. Now, Ralph, read a little from chapter 12 . . .

RALPH: "Something from the Spirit can be seen in each person, for the common good. The Spirit gives one person the ability to speak with wisdom, . . . "

GINNY *(to TED)*: That's you. Wait, did you give it to me or do you still have it?

RALPH: ". . . and the same Spirit gives another the ability to speak with knowledge."

MERYDITH *(to RALPH)*: That would be you.

RALPH: The same Spirit gives faith to one person.

CINDA: That's me . . .

RALPH: "And, to another, that one Spirit gives gifts of healing."

TED: No one has that yet.

GINNY *(to TOM)*: You can have it.

TOM: Wait. We're a little confused on . . .

GINNY: You don't want it? That's OK . . . you don't have to take it. Ralph gave his back . . . you can too.

TOM: I think we're a little confused. You can't choose a gift . . . it's given to you.

TED: Do we get a say?

TOM: No. It's a gift, chosen by the Holy Spirit . . . just for you.

CINDA: What if we don't want it?

TOM: You will . . . when you see . . .

MERYDITH: Can we just give some options?

TOM: No.

GINNY: So we just have to have faith we'll get what we want?

TOM: Well, yes.

RALPH: But wait, faith is a gift.

GINNY (*pointing at* CINDA): And she's got it.

RALPH: So if she's got it and we need it to get what's best for us, then how do we get a piece of it, or maybe a lot of it when it's not around to get? Or maybe that's a part of getting it because we have to have faith, but you can't just go get faith. It's either there or it's not. What do you say to that?

GINNY (*stands*): Oh . . . he just spoke in tongues!

(TOM *puts his head in his hands.*)

Blackout

The Game

by Jeff Smith

Scripture Reference: Philippians 3:14

Theme: Pressing on toward the goal

Cast (1 Male, 3 Males/Females):
PASTOR (M)
REPORTER 1 (M/F)
REPORTER 2 (M/F)
REPORTER 3 (M/F)

Setting: The scene is set up for an interview after a sporting event. There is a table and chair onstage. A glass of water is on the table.

Props:
Towel
Glass of water
3 pencils
3 notepads

Running Time: 4 minutes

(PASTOR *enters with towel draped around his neck and sits behind table. He wipes his brow and sighs. Looking like he's just played in a sporting event, he is seated before a roomful of reporters, ready to answer questions regarding the morning worship service. Scene should have the feel of a press conference after a sporting event. He wipes his brow and sips water throughout the interview. [Note: substitute names of people in the audience/congregation where appropriate.]*)

PASTOR: Before we open it up for questions, I want to say some things. I thought our people did a great job today. We had several new families visiting and we wanted to make a good impression. Our front line in the nursery was a little depleted with key players out, but we had some folks come off the pew and make some big plays in there. Our special teams, especially the ushers, were superb today. They have been working a couple new calls all week in practice and executed beautifully today. I saw Bill Bell make some moves on three or four defenders to find a couple of open seats in the front row for one new family. Greeters were playing one-on-one coverage, as usual, but Jim Palace saw a play break up a couple yards away from him and switched to zone coverage. You can't teach that. I mean they were reading handoffs and quick passes out there like bulletin inserts. I think most people were seated by the time we kicked things off with worship.

(REPORTERS, *seated in the audience/congregation, should stand to ask questions, taking notes as* PASTOR *responds.*)

REPORTER 1: What did you say to your team before the game?

PASTOR: We knew coming into today that we were going to have some troubles in that first quarter . . . uh, of an hour. We were missing our piano player, half of our front line in the choir, and two guys in the back row. Several families have condos in Florida, and they picked this weekend to start their vacations. That really hurt us. I'll be talking to their coordinator this week. I just wanted to get them to relax so I had them watch some clips from a Charles Stanley [Note: substitute the name of a familiar preacher.] service and the youth coordinator read some quotes from a Jack Hayford [Note: substitute the name of an inspirational leader.] book to get them fired up.

REPORTER 1: You obviously started out a little slow. Where did you feel like the momentum swung back to you?

PASTOR: Well, the children's message went well. You can drop the ball there and it will take a funny bounce. Once it's loose, it's anyone's game.

REPORTER 2: Someone on your special teams, Bob Brown, uh, I think he's an usher, was seen limping out of the service during greeting time. Is there any word on him?

PASTOR: Did you see the catch he made on the communion cup being passed between the rows? I mean it was a shoestring grab. Unbelievable! That catch saved us a time-out that would have really eaten up the clock. I'm sure that you'll be seeing that on the highlight films all week. But, we think he pulled a hamstring there. We'll check it out and see how serious the injury is. He'll be listed day to day.

REPORTER 3: There's speculation that your youth coordinator is leaving for a team of his own. Any truth to that?

PASTOR: I don't know where you guys get that stuff, you know? He has a team of his own right here and we don't want him to go anywhere. As you know, he was a first-round draft pick out of Messiah College, and we've been grooming him to move up with us. He's not going anywhere that I know.

REPORTER 2: Were you watching the clock on that last drive at the end of the sermon?

PASTOR: We approach every play like time is running out for someone. But, I can't play the clock. We try and keep things moving.

REPORTER 1: Did you make that last call?

PASTOR: The altar call? I think everyone here knows that we have a pretty hands-on Coach. He makes that call. We just execute. My job is to keep it close so that we can win in the last five minutes or so. I try to be in a position to air it out there and hope that someone comes up big with it.

REPORTER 3: Now that you've got these victories under your belt, are you looking ahead to *[Note: feel free to substitute the next big service.]* Easter?

PASTOR: Really, we can't afford to look past next week. We had two souls saved today. That's a big win for our side. But we can't afford to underestimate the opponent from week to week. The stakes are just too high. But we are going to enjoy the victory today. So, if you folks will excuse me . . . (PASTOR *gets up to exit.*)

REPORTER 1: Nice game out there, Pastor.

PASTOR *(stops and turns):* Game? What made you think we were playing a game? This is war.

Blackout

Like a Bad Neighbor

by Martha Bolton

Scripture References: "If you really keep the royal law found in Scripture, 'Love your neighbor as yourself,' you are doing right" (James 2:8); the Parable of the Good Samaritan (Luke 10:29-37).

Themes: Kindness; Loving your neighbor as yourself

Cast:
> ESOM
> MICAH—Insurance agent for Samaritan's Life

Setting: The road between Jerusalem and Jericho

Props:
> Table
> Two chairs
> Papers
> Customer card
> Speech card
> Two items that look like policies

Costumes: Biblical era wear or jeans and a T-shirt with a cloth draped over the shoulder, biblical era style.

Running time: 5-6 minutes

(Opens with MICAH *and* ESOM *sitting at a table. We join them mid sales pitch. Papers, policies, and cards are on the table in front of* MICAH.*)*

MICAH: Yes, yes, I realize you're only shopping for home insurance, but I wouldn't be doing my job if I didn't tell you about our newest, most comprehensive policy.

ESOM: Thanks, but I'm on a limited budget. Medicare won't kick in for another 2,000 years or so, and I've really got to start watching my expenses.

MICAH: And we here at Samaritan's Life appreciate that. That's why we've priced our policies very modestly.

ESOM: How modestly?

MICAH: We'll get to that later.

ESOM: Let's get to that now.

MICAH: We can do that, but you'd be throwing off my pacing.

ESOM: Pacing?

MICAH: My prescripted memorized speech. Throw off the pacing and it won't sound natural and convincing. You won't "trust" me. And our company is built on trust.

ESOM: Look, I really don't think I'm interested in . . .

MICAH: We treat our customers like family, Mr. *(reading name from speech card)* Fill in Name . . .

ESOM: Esom.

MICAH: Esom, right now you're probably saying to yourself, Mr. Insurance Man, I have insurance for my house, insurance for my chariot, but I don't have a policy that covers me when I'm out walking on these dangerous highways . . .

ESOM: Actually, I was telling myself how I don't have time for . . .

MICAH *(continuing without missing a beat)*: We know all about your insurance concerns, Esom . . . friend . . . brother . . . and we don't want you fretting over them another second, because we've got the answer right here . . . *(holds up paper)*

ESOM *(reading from paper that MICAH is waving)*: Your plumbing bill?

MICAH *(looking at paper, reacts)*: I mean, here . . . *(Holds up real policy)* Our Good Samaritan's policy will cover you wherever your feet take you.

ESOM: Right now my feet just want to take me home.

MICAH: And you'd be covered . . . if you take out a policy today.

ESOM: I don't need insurance to walk.

MICAH: That depends on where you're walking, bro.

ESOM: This is a good neighborhood. What could happen?

MICAH: Don't you read the papers?

ESOM: I'm a busy man, which is why I really need to be . . . *(starts to rise)*

MICAH: Well, then, you obviously didn't hear about the man who was walking from Jerusalem to Jericho the other night . . .

ESOM: No. But I have a feeling you're going to tell me.

MICAH: He was robbed, stripped of his clothes, and left by the side of the road to die! Esom . . . buddy . . . pal . . . "E" . . . that could've been you!

ESOM: Boy, you insurance people sure like the scare tactics, don't you?

MICAH: I'm just a realist.

ESOM: A guy's killed by a bunch of robbers and . . .

MICAH: Who said he died?

ESOM: You did.

MICAH: I didn't say he died.

ESOM: Yes, you did.

MICAH: I said he was left by the side of the road to die.

ESOM: So he's OK?

MICAH: Did I say that?

ESOM: So what happened?

MICAH: If I didn't have so many interruptions, I could get through this.

ESOM: All right. Go on.

MICAH *(looking at speech card)*: Now, where was I? . . . Oh, yeah. The man was left there bleeding by the side of the road and a priest happened by . . .

ESOM: The priest took him to the hospital and all's well that ends well. *(Rising)* Now, if you'll excuse me . . .

MICAH: The priest didn't take him anywhere.

ESOM *(sitting back down)*: He didn't?

MICAH: Nope.

ESOM: Did he at least pray for him?

MICAH: If he did, he did it from the other side of the street. You see, "E," . . . it's not safe out there. You need protection! You need us!

ESOM: But I thought you said the guy didn't die.

MICAH: I'm not through yet. A Levite came by next.

ESOM: And he helped him?

MICAH: No. And you're not helping me much either. Now, let me finish the story the way I'm supposed to. *(Reading from speech card)* "A Levite came by next . . . "

ESOM: You said that already.

MICAH: You never got the "Good Listener" sticker in school, did you?

ESOM: Come on, man, cut to the chase.

MICAH *(reading from speech card, slowly and deliberately)*: "The Levite came by and pretended the guy wasn't even there either."

ESOM: You're telling me that this guy is lying by the side of the road, half-dead. The religious leader doesn't help him, the Levite doesn't help him . . . nobody helps him?

MICAH: They didn't want to get involved. Nobody helped him. Until finally, a Samaritan came by . . .

ESOM: Uh-oh. He's in trouble now. (MICAH *gives him a look for interrupting.*) Sorry, but a guy from Jerusalem and a Samaritan? They're enemies, aren't they? So when's the guy's funeral? (MICAH *continues looking.* ESOM *responds apologetically.*) OK, OK. I'll be quiet.

MICAH: The Samaritan was the only one who showed compassion for the guy, but that's not the point of the story.

ESOM: Sounds like the point to me—sometimes our help comes from a place where we least expect it.

MICAH: The point is you can't trust anyone to help you out in your time of trouble . . . no one but Samaritan's Life. We're here when you need us.

ESOM: So if you had walked by, you would have helped the guy?

MICAH: Are you kidding? Put my life in danger? No. But as soon as the guy was able to fill out these forms (*holds up huge stack*), we would have happily reimbursed 14 percent of his medical bills. That's the point of the story. When you're in trouble, we're here to help.

ESOM: So how much of the man's bills did this Samaritan guy pay?

MICAH: A hundred percent, but you're getting me off message here.

ESOM: A hundred percent? And he didn't even know him?

MICAH: Let's stay on track here, bro. I shared this story with you so you'd see why you need the Good Samaritan's policy. You never know what's going to happen to you out on these roads, and you can't always count on others to help.

ESOM: The Good Samaritan's policy isn't the answer. The answer is more good Samaritans.

MICAH: I'm afraid they're almost extinct. So here . . . (*sliding policy across table to him*) sign right here on the dotted line and your coverage will begin immediately.

ESOM: Thanks, but . . . (*rising to leave*) no thanks.

MICAH: It was my speech, wasn't it? I'll do it again . . . this time without all your interruptions. I can be a lot more convincing. Wait . . . it was that anecdote. It wasn't very funny. I knew I should've opened with a joke. You're always supposed to open with a joke. But not me! Nooooo. I had to go for the drama!

ESOM: It wasn't your speech. It's just that I choose to believe there's some good left in people.

MICAH *(laughing uncontrollably):* Come on, really, why won't you sign it?

ESOM *(rising):* I really do need to be going.

MICAH: All right, suit yourself. But when you're left by the side of the road, and everyone you thought was going to help you walks right on by, don't say we at Samaritan's Life didn't warn you! I'm telling ya, people just don't want to get involved anymore.

ESOM: Well, maybe it's time a few more of us started changing that.

MICAH *(laughs skeptically):* Yeah . . . right. Like a handful of good Samaritans is going to make a difference in this self-centered world.

ESOM: It only took one good Samaritan to make a difference in that man's life. Just one. And who knows, maybe the idea'll catch on. *(Exiting)* See ya . . . "bro."

MICAH: Uh . . . yeah . . . see ya *(glances down at customer card),* . . . Esom. (MICAH *watches* ESOM *leave, left alone in thought.)*

Blackout

Majority Rules

by Chuck Neighbors

Scripture Reference: Romans 1:18-32

Themes: Truth; Relativism; Absolutes

Cast:
    JUDGE BENJAMIN FICKLE—Absent-minded professor type
    JAMES CAPRICE—Lawyer for the defense
    SALLY STRIKER—Prosecuting attorney
    ALICE WRIGHT—Defendant
    BAILIFF—Very official
    MESSENGER—A walk-on, no lines

Props:
    Gavel
    A large official-looking book
    Dictionary
    File folders and papers

Setting: A courtroom on the fictional Island of Cretin. CS are a judge's bench and the witness stand. SL, facing right, is the prosecutor's table and a chair. On SR, facing left, is the defense table with two chairs.

Note: This play is meant to be played broadly and for laughs. The pretext is absurd. It is in the total absurdity of the play that the point will be made. Don't be overly concerned about proper courtroom procedure. Have fun!

Running Time: 8 minutes

(*Opens with* CAPRICE, WRIGHT, *and* STRIKER *already onstage and in their proper places.* BAILIFF *enters.*)

BAILIFF (*crossing to CS*): All rise. (*Cast stands.*) Hear ye, hear ye. This court is now in session. The Honorable Judge Benjamin Fickle presiding.

(JUDGE FICKLE *enters, crossing to CS behind judge's bench, sits.*)

BAILIFF (*after* FICKLE *sits*): Be seated. (*Moves to side*)

FICKLE: The court calls the case of the Island of Cretin vs. Alice Wright. Is the defendant present and with counsel?

CAPRICE (*standing*): She is, Your Honor. James Caprice for the defense. (*Sits*)

FICKLE: Is the prosecution present and ready to present its case?

STRIKER *(standing):* I am, Your Honor. Sally Striker, representing the Island of Cretin. *(Sits)*

FICKLE: Will the defendant please rise? (WRIGHT *and* CAPRICE *both stand.)* Alice Wright, you have been charged with speaking a forbidden language. Current law prohibits speaking in any language other than English on the Island of Cretin. How do you plead?

(WRIGHT *looks unsure.* CAPRICE *whispers something to* WRIGHT, *who then speaks.)*

WRIGHT: Not guilty, Your Honor.

FICKLE: Very well. Be seated. *(They sit.)* Prosecution, you may present your case.

STRIKER *(standing):* Thank you, Your Honor. The prosecution would like to call the defendant, Alice Wright, to the stand.

CAPRICE *(standing):* Objection. The defendant cannot be called to testify against herself.

STRIKER: Your Honor, that rule was changed. If you will refer to the Daily Law Change Log, the majority overturned that rule by a narrow margin just yesterday.

FICKLE *(looking through book):* You're right. Overruled. Bailiff, swear in the defendant.

(CAPRICE *sits as* WRIGHT *moves, nervously, to CS and is met by* BAILIFF.)

BAILIFF: Do you swear to tell the truth or the relative truth or the truth whatever you perceive it to be?

WRIGHT *(a bit confused):* I . . . uh . . . think so . . . I—

BAILIFF: A simple "whatever" will suffice.

WRIGHT: Uh . . . whatever.

BAILIFF: You may be seated. (WRIGHT *sits.* BAILIFF *moves to side.)*

FICKLE: Your witness, Ms. Striker.

STRIKER: Thank you, Your Honor. Ms. Wright, on the evening of Saturday, August 7, an acquaintance of a friend of a friend of yours told an unnamed source of ours that you were overheard to be speaking to a tourist on our beloved Island of Cretin.

CAPRICE *(on his feet):* Objection! Hearsay, Your Honor.

STRIKER: Hearsay is now admissible as evidence, Your Honor. I refer you to the Daily Law Change Log for Monday of last week. The majority voted to change the rules on last week's voting docket.

FICKLE *(checking book):* Quite right, Ms. Striker. Overruled. You may continue.

STRIKER: Do you acknowledge that this conversation took place?

WRIGHT: I am not sure of the date, but yes, I did speak to a tourist several weeks ago.

STRIKER: Do you recall where this tourist was from, Ms. Wright?

WRIGHT: Yes, he was from Hogland.

STRIKER: And do you know what language they speak in Hogland, Ms. Wright.

WRIGHT: They speak English.

STRIKER: That is not what I understand, Ms. Wright. Our research indicates that the official language of Hogland is not English, but Pig Latin!

WRIGHT: Yes, but—

STRIKER: Did you speak to this tourist in English or Pig Latin?

WRIGHT: Well . . . Uh . . . I—

STRIKER: English or Pig Latin, Ms. Wright?

WRIGHT: Well, let me explain—

STRIKER: Just answer the question. English or Pig Latin?

CAPRICE (standing): Objection, Your Honor. The prosecution is badgering the witness.

FICKLE: Yes, yes. Sustained. That law has not been changed recently. I am aware that there was an effort to allow badgering in a vote last month but the majority did not approve it.

STRIKER: Your Honor, I do not perceive that I am badgering the witness. The truth, as I perceive it to be, is simply to get an answer from this reluctant witness. Your Honor will recall that we hold sacred the truth, as *each person* perceives it.

FICKLE (pausing to think): Why, you are quite right. Forgive me. Overruled.

CAPRICE: I must object, Your Honor. The truth, as I perceive it, is that the prosecution was badgering the witness.

FICKLE: Then, you are quite right. If you perceive that the witness is being badgered, then you are sustained.

STRIKER: Your Honor, I must object. We can't both be right.

FICKLE: Of course you can. The truth is, and always will be, relative to each person's perception of the truth—unless the law changes again. However, to settle this little dispute we will put it to a vote. Will all those in the court who think the witness is being badgered, raise your hand. (CAPRICE *and* WRIGHT *raise their hands as* FICKLE *counts.*) One, two. All those who think the witness is not being badgered, raise your hands. (STRIKER, BAILIFF, *and* FICKLE *raise their hands.*) One, two, three. Vote is three to two. The witness was not being badgered. Ms. Striker, you may continue.

STRIKER: Thank you, Your Honor. Answer the question, Ms. Wright.

WRIGHT: Uh, I'm sorry . . . I have forgotten the question.

STRIKER: The question, Ms. Wright, was were you speaking to the tourist in English or Pig Latin?

WRIGHT: Pig Latin. But—

STRIKER: Thank you, Ms. Wright. No further questions, Your Honor. *(Sits)*

FICKLE: Very well. Does the defense have any questions for the witness?

CAPRICE: Yes, Your Honor. *(Standing)* Ms. Wright, you have testified that you did indeed speak to this tourist in Pig Latin. How is it that you know how to speak Pig Latin?

WRIGHT: I was born in Hogland. My parents are Hoglandians. Pig Latin is my native tongue.

CAPRICE: Can you tell the court why you were speaking in Pig Latin to this tourist?

WRIGHT: He was lost. He had some trouble with formal English, so I thought I could be of help by speaking to him in his native tongue.

STRIKER *(standing):* Objection, Your Honor. The witness's motives are not relevant to this case.

CAPRICE: I disagree, Your Honor. It is my intention to establish that the defendant was in the act of performing a good deed—

STRIKER: I object, Your Honor. Good deeds are no longer permissible on Cretin, due to the agony that they cause the majority—who suffer from the guilt inflicted by their own lack of performing same.

CAPRICE: If the prosecution will allow me to finish! I am fully aware that good deeds are illegal. My intention is to establish that the defendant is a *victim* in this case. She is not responsible for her good deeds, but is, rather, responding to patterns established in her childhood by parents who were fanatical in their obsession for doing good. Your Honor, I will establish that the defendant's parents were do-gooding deed-aholics, and as such, she cannot be held accountable for her actions!

FICKLE *(flipping through book):* Mr. Caprice, I applaud your resourcefulness. That line of defense would have worked three weeks ago. However, the new laws, allowing victimization of criminals as a line of defense, excludes do-gooding as a valid approach. The majority simply does not want anything to do with this guilt-inducing contaminate to our society. Objection sustained! Mr. Caprice, you will please pursue another line of questioning.

CAPRICE *(sighs):* Very well, Your Honor. Ms. Wright, did you know that it was against Cretin law to speak any language other than English?

WRIGHT: Yes.

CAPRICE: Why, then, did you knowingly and willingly speak Pig Latin?

WRIGHT: That is what I was trying to tell the court before. Pig Latin *is* English. It is just another form of the language—a jargon, if you will.

STRIKER *(standing):* I object, Your Honor. Is the defendant an expert on the English language? If not, her testimony should be considered opinion, not fact.

FICKLE: Overruled. Opinion is considered fact under current Cretin law.

CAPRICE: Thank you, Your Honor. However, if it please the court, I also submit that the words found in Webster's Dictionary also support this opinion. It reads, and I quote: "Pig Latin: A jargon that is made by systematic mutilation of English." Your Honor, as Webster points out, Pig Latin—although a mutilation—is indeed a jargon of the English language. In view of both this opinion as well as *fact*, I request that the charges be dropped against my client.

(Messenger enters carrying a note to BAILIFF, *who reads it silently while* FICKLE *says next line.)*

FICKLE: It is fortunate for your client that this case is being tried at this time and not tomorrow. Today mutilation is legal—tomorrow it becomes illegal. Case dismissed.

BAILIFF: Excuse me, Your Honor?

FICKLE: Yes, what is it?

BAILIFF: I have just received an urgent message about a law that will take effect immediately. I think you had better read it.

FICKLE: Let me see. *(Takes paper, reads aloud)* "In the interest of diversity, and as a gesture of understanding toward minorities, the majority has just ruled that as of 12 noon today, the new official language of Cretin will be Pig Latin. Anyone caught speaking any other language, jargon, or form of English after 12 noon today will be arrested and brought to trial." 12 noon. *(Looking at watch)* Good heavens—that's in 5 seconds.

(Expressions of disbelief as all look at their watches and wait)

FICKLE: Isthay ourtcay isay ownay adjourneday.
    ("This court is now adjourned.")

STRIKER: But Your Honor, I object. I don't know how to speak Pig Latin.

FICKLE: Ailiffbay, arrestay Izmay Ikerstray.
("Bailiff, arrest Ms. Striker.")

(BAILIFF *moves to arrest* STRIKER.)

STRIKER: But Your Honor!

FICKLE: Aketay erhay awayay!
("Take her away!")

BAILIFF: Ou'reyay underay arrestay. Omecay ithway emay, adylay.
("You're under arrest. Come with me, lady.")

(FICKLE, BAILIFF *and* STRIKER, *still protesting, exit.*)

WRIGHT: Ymay, ymay. Iay eelfay orrysay orfay erhay. Aybemay Iay ouldcay elphay erhay earnlay Igpay Atinlay.
("My, my. I feel sorry for her. Maybe I could help her learn Pig Latin.")

CAPRICE: Ownay, ownay. Onay oremay oodgay eedsday. Ellway, ouyay onway. Et'slay elebratecay!
("Now, now. No more good deeds. Well, you won. Let's celebrate!")

WRIGHT: Esyay, et'slay! Anday anksthay orfay everythingay.
("Yes, let's! And thanks for everything.") (Exiting)

Ethay Enday
(The End)

Joy to the World

by Jeff Smith

Scripture Reference: Psalm 100:4

Theme: Entering into the presence of God should bring joy.

Cast (2 Males/2 Females):
    CHAD (Male 30 plus)—Gruff, football fanatic
    DIANE (Female 20 plus)—Single and actively looking not to be
    BETH (Female 40 plus)—Self-absorbed and preoccupied
    FRANK (Male 40 plus)—Needy thespian

Setting: Four people in a row or pew are singing the hymn, "Joy to the World." But what we hear them sing is what they are thinking as they sing the song.

Props:
    4 hymnals
    Hand purse

Running Time: 2 minutes

(To the tune of the traditional hymn "Joy to the World." When characters are not singing their solo lines, they should be mouthing the words to the traditional hymn.)

ALL: "Joy to the world! the Lord is come;"

FRANK: I get to play the king.

CHAD: The Redskins play the Bills at four.

BETH: Did I forget to lock the door?

DIANE: Who is that guy over there? With the blue eyes and blonde hair?

ALL: "And heav'n . . ."

DIANE: Good heavens, we'd make quite a pair.

ALL: "Joy to the world! the Savior reigns;"

CHAD: Let Norv *[Note: substitute name of the coach of a professional sports team.]* be unemployed.

FRANK: I'll know my lines when we rehearse.

BETH *(fumbling through purse):* My car keys are not in my purse.

DIANE: Perhaps if I can sneeze, he will look my way, oh please

29

ALL: "Repeat,"

CHAD: Reheat the nachos and the cheese.

ALL: "No more let sin and sorrow grow, Nor thorns infest . . ."

DIANE: Aaaachooo! *(Sneezes)*

FRANK: I'll act like Good King Wenceslas, and get to carry frankincense.

BETH: I feel like such a jerk.

DIANE: He looked at me. It worked!

CHAD: If the Bills beat the Redskins, I will go bezerk. *[Note: change names of teams to local sports team, if necessary.]*

ALL: "He rules the world with truth and grace,"

FRANK: The director will approve.

CHAD: I hope the sermon's short and sweet.

BETH *(now crawling under pews/chairs):* Perhaps they fell beneath my seat.

DIANE: He looked at me and winked. All my bridesmaids will wear pink.

ALL: And you wonder, you wonder what the Lord must think. *[Note: Slow down the singing of the very last line to add emphasis.]*

The End

I Feel like a Punching Bag

by Jim Custer and Bob Hoose

Scripture References: Romans 5:1-5; Isaiah 40:28-31

Theme: Spiritual Dryness and Difficulties of Life

Cast:
> KEVIN—A man about 38 years old, quietly discouraged
> SHERRY—His wife, who is his soul mate and uses a backdoor kind of logic
> JACK—Their son, about 12 to 14; an offstage voice

Setting: The Matthews' garage

Props:
> A bounce-back punching bag
> One or two basketfuls of clothes
> The sound of a bouncing basketball
> A broom

Lighting: Basic wash with a quick fade

Running Time: 6 minutes

Suggestions:
> Begin the scene with a short musical rift that says "suburbia." Use the same rift at the end. Pastor could come out after the sketch is over, punch the punching bag, and say "Do you ever feel like life treats you like a punching bag?"

(Opens with KEVIN punching a child's stand-up punching bag. SHERRY enters with a basket of clothes. Throughout the scene she can separate the clothes as if she is getting ready to do a wash.)

SHERRY: Thinking of my mother again?

KEVIN: No, just cleaning up the garage. Found this. It's Jack's. Still holds air. *(Throws a hard punch)*

SHERRY: Not for long.

KEVIN: You know, this is really therapeutic.

SHERRY: What's going on, sweetheart?

KEVIN: Ah, nothing . . . just cleaning the garage. *(Punches bag again)*

SHERRY: Now come on, Muhammad Ali, you can do better than that. You've been preoccupied since Tuesday. Something at work?

31

KEVIN: I'm fine. *(Starts dancing around punch toy like a boxer)* I'm floating like a butterfly and stinging like a bee. *(Punches at toy and misses)*

SHERRY: Kevin . . .

KEVIN: He ducked.

SHERRY: Kevin . . .

KEVIN: I better get this place cleaned up. *(Exits to get broom)*

SHERRY *(to KEVIN as he exits):* This all started on Tuesday. What happened on Tuesday?

KEVIN *(entering with broom and box):* Maybe we should have a garage sale. (SHERRY *just looks at him.*) What? It's nothing, hon. I'll work it out.

SHERRY: It?

KEVIN: Spiritual stuff.

SHERRY: Spiritual stuff?

KEVIN: Are you just going to stand there and repeat me? (SHERRY *stares at him.*) OK. OK. Oprah, . . . I'll talk. Women and their "communication thing." Monday night, when Charlie was doing . . .

SHERRY: At care group? (KEVIN *gives her a look.*) Sorry.

KEVIN: Charlie said we should always know the joy of the Lord. No matter what is going on in our lives, no matter what the turmoil, there should still be that inner joy and peace. If we take the time to pray, at least 30 minutes of uninterrupted communication with Christ, then followed by meditation in the Word, we will always have that reservoir of "God centeredness."

SHERRY: So?

KEVIN: So, someone drained my reservoir. It's a dust bowl in there and all the fish are dead. Well, at least compared to Charlie.

SHERRY: And this is what's bugging you.

KEVIN: Well, that and I feel old. I'm starting to lose hair . . .

SHERRY: You are not.

KEVIN: I woke up this morning and my pillow looked like a Chia pet. It won't be long and I'll have more hair in my ears than on my head.

SHERRY: You have a full head of hair. *(Rubbing her hand through it)*

KEVIN: It might look full, but believe me, the troops are getting ready to go AWOL. Added to that . . . work stinks. I feel as useful as a stump. Then, Jack.

SHERRY: What's wrong with Jack?

KEVIN: He gets this deer-in-the-headlights look and starts hyperventilating whenever I get near him and his friends.

SHERRY: All kids go through that stage.

KEVIN: Yeah, well it bugs me. I feel . . . I feel . . . "Is this all there is? Is this what life is supposed to be?" The only thing that could top it all off is me passing a kidney stone while getting a root canal. (SHERRY *stares at him.*) You asked for it. *(Beat)* So when Charlie started preaching . . . I said to myself . . . "Self, what's wrong? Why don't you have that inner joy and peace? Maybe you're not doing something right. Maybe you got some deep seated sin somewhere. Maybe you ticked God off somehow." I don't know. *(Punches bag)*

SHERRY: Well, maybe you're right. Maybe you have blown it somehow.

KEVIN: Now I'm feeling better.

SHERRY: Seriously, you might not be saved.

KEVIN: What? I'm saved. When I was 18, I asked Christ into my life. I was baptized. I know I'm saved.

SHERRY: Maybe it didn't take.

KEVIN: This isn't like coloring your hair and having it come out blue. I know I'm saved.

SHERRY: Then maybe God doesn't like you very much.

KEVIN: That's scriptural. God loved the world, except Kevin Matthews, so much that He sent His only begotten Son . . .

SHERRY: It was just a thought. Maybe if you were a better father. You could work on that.

KEVIN: Work on it? I work on it every day! There isn't anything I wouldn't do for Jack. You know that!

SHERRY: Still . . .

KEVIN: What?

SHERRY: I'm just saying, you're not making any kind of . . . impact on this world. What kind of legacy are you leaving?

KEVIN: You're joking.

SHERRY: Bupkis.

KEVIN: That's not . . .

SHERRY: A big goose egg.

KEVIN: I'll have you know I . . .

SHERRY: Nada.

KEVIN: In my Sunday School class . . .

SHERRY: You got a big bucket but it's empty . . .

KEVIN: In my Sunday School class I had the kids draw a picture of Jesus and you know what?

SHERRY: The doughnut is one big hole.

KEVIN: Brandon James drew a picture of me, well . . . the hair was green and he only had one eye, but Brandon said, "Mr. Matthews, you're like Jesus." Now what does that say?

SHERRY (*turning and looking at him*): What does that say? (KEVIN *looks at her, slowly beginning to catch on.*) God chose you. I chose you. Neither one of us is sorry for the decision. So, you don't do it like Charlie. I didn't see the Good Heaven Seal of Approval on his handouts. You are . . . a part of God's eternal dream. Nothing can stop that. And I am the luckiest woman in the world. I love you now . . . and I'll love you when you're bald and all your hair has moved to your ears.

KEVIN (*kissing her*): Sort'a like Chicken Soup for Those Who Clean Garages.

SHERRY: We all go through those times when we feel like life has punched us around a little. That's why we need each other to be the sand in the bottom of the bag.

KEVIN: The what?

SHERRY: You know the sand in the bottom of the punching bag . . . that helps it . . . (*Tries to demonstrate, gives up*) OK, I took the metaphor a little far. You know what I mean. (*They laugh and hug.*)

JACK (*offstage*): Hey, Dad. You wanna play a little one-on-one?

KEVIN: He recognized my existence.

SHERRY: Better hurry, it could be just a hiccup.

KEVIN (*to* JACK): I'll be right there. Thanks, Hon. (*Kisses her again, exits*)

SHERRY (*watches him go, walks over to punching bag, and gives it a smack*): Huh. It is therapeutic.

Blackout

T-Shirts

by Chuck Neighbors

Scripture References: Matthew 5:43-48; Matthew 6:1-24

Theme: A tongue-in-cheek look at the commercial side of Christian pop culture

Cast:
> JERRY

Props:
> Shirts and hats for sale
> A cloth "friendship" bracelet

Running Time: 4 minutes

(A Christian music festival—specifically the tent where all the vendors sell their wares. As lights come up, JERRY is working the crowd. He straightens up shirts and hats on a table and/or on hangers on racks. The business with shirts can be done with real props or in pantomime. JERRY should keep busy with props throughout the monologue. Though a monologue, be sure to allow "listening" to other imagined characters with appropriate pauses.)

JERRY: Buy your shirts! Christian shirts here! Any two shirts for 25 bucks. Get your Christian hats here! We have the best selection. Hey . . . hey . . . you. Yeah, I like your shirt. That's great! Kinda a good reminder, isn't it? You wear that shirt and people know where you stand. We don't sell that one anymore—that one's kinda run its course. There are others out there now. We have the best selection of all the vendors here at the Solid Rock Christian Music Festival. Take a look at these new shirts. *(Getting shirts to show "customer")* We got the F.R.O.G.s over here . . . Oh, you haven't seen that one? Lookie here, I got one of them friendship bracelets with that on it.

    F.R.O.G. . . . You don't know what it means? That means Fully Relying on God. F.R.O.G. Good reminder, isn't it?. Sort of tells everybody where you stand. Why, today, when I see a frog, it just naturally makes me think of God. Of course, it should be that way with everything, don't you think? I mean, God made everything so everything we see should make us think of God. But now, man, it's F.R.O.G.s. Frogs and God, man. Ain't it great?!

    Oh, we got the shirts of all the kids' favorite groups. We got your Supertones, Newsboys, D.C.Talk, Five Iron Frenzy, and even that P.O.D. Pod?! I don't know what that one means. Funny name, but hey, the kids really go for it. Over here we have the parody shirts. Here is one patterned after the logo of that show "Survivor," only ours says "Savior" in the middle. Oh, this one here is real popular, you know the Budweiser "What's-up?" commercial? *(Imitating commercial)* Whaaaasuupppp? Well, look at

35

this one, it says "Lookup," then you have your cross on a hillside—the Cross, that makes it Christian, ya know—and then it says "Be-Wiser" at the bottom. Looooookuuuuup! Kinda cool, huh? It's so great that you can witness with these things. You don't have to say anything. Just let the shirt do the talking. They see your shirt and they know where you stand. Great way to share your faith.

'Course, sometimes it gets turned around a bit. I mean, like everybody wears a cross, Christian or not. Even Madonna wears a cross. Whaaaassupp with that? (Laughs) And like with your "W.W.J.D.?" "What Would Jesus Do?" My name's Jerry so my wife, Janice, always says, "What Would Jerry Do?" I kinda tease her back and say, yeah, well, "What would Janice do?" We sell them "W.W.J.D.?" bracelets with the block letters and one of 'em was messed up. It had too many Ws and no J. W.W.W.D.? Some guy bought it anyway. His name was Walter. What would Walter do? Kinda funny, eh?

I saw one that kinda bothered me. Not here at the Festival, but at the Mall back in Portland. Some kid was wearing a shirt that said W.W.J.D. and I thought "hey great, a Christian brother," ya know. Then I walked up to him and was about to say "hi" when I noticed that underneath the W.W.J.D. it said "Water with Jack Daniels." Ticked me off, man! What a shame. They take something like that and make fun of it. Made me want to punch him, ya know. Kinda like those Darwin-eating-the-fish bumper stickers. Makes me want to ram right into them with my truck. I hate it when people make fun of our witness, ya know.

I saw some of the NBA players wearing the "W.W.J.D.?" bracelets. I'm thinking that, hey, they must be Christians, ya know. Then the next day I read in the papers where this guy—one of the same NBA players I seen on the tube, wearing a bracelet—gets busted for drugs and carrying a gun and all that. Ticks me off. Kinda tarnishes the image, you know what I mean?

Hey, sorry, didn't mean to talk your ear off . . . Sure, you just go ahead and browse. Let me know if you see something you like. I'll make you a good deal.

(Talking to other customers)

Buy your shirts here! Christian hats. Christian shirts. Any two shirts for $25. Hi, how ya doin'?

(Walks away and "sees" first "customer")

Hey! Hey you! Come back here with that. Stop that man! He is stealing from me! Did you see that! He just stole a "Lookup" T-shirt . . . That guy running over there . . . No, the guy I was just talking to. About my height. He was wearing a tan hat and a white T-shirt that had "W.W.J.D.?" on it. Janice, call Security! We lost another shirt! ARRGGHHH!

(Lights fade.)

The End

Like a Mustard Seed

by Martha Bolton

Scripture References:

"He told them another parable: 'The kingdom of heaven is like a mustard seed, which a man took and planted in his field'" (Matthew 13:31).

"He replied, 'Because you have so little faith. I tell you the truth, if you have faith as small as a mustard seed, you can say to this mountain, "Move from here to there" and it will move. Nothing will be impossible for you'" (Matthew 17:20).

"It is like a mustard seed, which is the smallest seed you plant in the ground" (Mark 4:31).

"It is like a mustard seed, which a man took and planted in his garden. It grew and became a tree, and the birds of the air perched in its branches" (Luke 13:19).

"He replied, 'If you have faith as small as a mustard seed, you can say to this mulberry tree, "Be uprooted and planted in the sea," and it will obey you'" (Luke 17:6).

Theme: Faith

Description:

A husband and wife wake up one morning to discover the incredible faith of a mustard seed.

Cast:

MARILYN
HAROLD

Setting: Upstairs bedroom of their two-story home

Props:

Treetop (should look as though it has broken its way up through the floor)
Bird nest (in treetop)
Bed (two rollaways or two cots would work easily)
Dirty sock
(*Note: Treetop and bird nest are optional and can be imagined rather than real.*)

Costumes: Modern-day wear

Running time: 5 minutes

(*Opens with* MARILYN *waking up. She crawls out of bed and is surprised by the "tree-top" sticking up through a newly created "hole" in the middle of the floor.* HAROLD *is sound asleep in the cot or bed next to her.*)

MARILYN: Harold . . . Harold! Get up and take a look at this!

HAROLD: What? (*Grumpily stumbles out of bed, half asleep, sees treetop and "hole"*) What in the world?

MARILYN: It's a tree.

HAROLD: I can see that. What's it doing in our bedroom?

MARILYN: It must've pushed its way up through the second-story floor while we were sleeping.

HAROLD: Oh. (*Walks back to bed, climbs in, and rolls over to go back to sleep*)

MARILYN: Harold!

HAROLD: What?!

MARILYN: Aren't you going to do anything about it?

HAROLD: What do you want me to do? Start looking around for Jack?

MARILYN: Very funny. This isn't a beanstalk, and no one's laying a golden egg.

HAROLD: Then why do I hear so much cackling?

MARILYN: I'm gonna ignore that.

HAROLD (*unenthusiastically crawls out of bed*): Oh, all right. You just hate to see me get any rest at all, don't you, woman?

MARILYN: The rain forest is growing in our bedroom, and all you can think about is sleep?!

HAROLD: You're the one who insisted on having houseplants!

MARILYN: How was I supposed to know this would happen? What are we gonna do?

HAROLD: I don't know, but until we figure it out, I'd lay off the Miracle Grow.

MARILYN: I didn't use any Miracle Grow.

HAROLD: So then . . . this is an act of God.

MARILYN: God wanted us to have a tree in our bedroom?

HAROLD: Maybe He's trying to tell us something.

MARILYN: Like what?

HAROLD: Like maybe you need to sweep the floors a little more often.

MARILYN: I'm sure God knows that the broom works just as well when you operate it, too, dear.

HAROLD: OK, so that's not what He's trying to tell us.

MARILYN: Look, for some reason, there's a tree growing in our house. We've got a problem, and we'll just have to figure out how to take care of it. WWMSD.

HAROLD: WWMSD?

MARILYN: Would Would Martha Stewart Do?

HAROLD: Something tells me she probably doesn't have a book on this particular problem. *(Examining tree)* So, what kind of tree you figure it is anyway?

MARILYN: Well, it's not a maple.

HAROLD: It's not a magnolia.

MARILYN: You don't think this is that mustard seed I planted awhile back, do you?

HAROLD: That itty bitty thing? No way.

MARILYN: But that's the only plant I haven't been checking on. The kids have been watering it for me.

HAROLD: Can a mustard seed do . . . this?

MARILYN: I've heard people talk about having the faith of a mustard seed. Maybe this is what they mean.

HAROLD: So maybe that's why it's here. God's trying to teach us about faith.

MARILYN: He couldn't have just had a preacher stop by?

HAROLD: The Lord works in mysterious ways . . . Hey, look. We could use it as a laundry rack. *(Tosses dirty sock on it)*

MARILYN: Oh, yeah, that's just what we need—a dirty sock tree.

HAROLD: That's it! "The Dirty Sock Tree!" We could sell a million of these on eBay! God is saying He wants us to be RICH!

MARILYN: You need help.

HAROLD: Of course, I'll need help. Someone has to keep track of the bids, the closing date of the auction . . .

MARILYN: If God did do this, I don't think it was so we could sell Dirty Sock Trees on eBay.

HAROLD: What's He got against eBay?

MARILYN: Probably nothing. But that's not my point. My point is we're getting to see firsthand how big the faith of a mustard seed is.

HAROLD: Our insurance company is never going to believe this.

MARILYN: Maybe this happened to us so we can tell others that Jesus was right . . .

if you have the faith of just a little mustard seed, look at what all you can accomplish.

HAROLD: So we should call the paper then?

MARILYN: The paper, *Newsweek*, Bill O'Reilly . . . maybe we could even enter it in the state fair.

HAROLD: A blue ribbon winner for sure!

MARILYN: And we can't forget about the best way of all to get the message out.

HAROLD: What's that?

MARILYN: Well, since it's almost Christmas, whatd'ya say we decorate it and leave it right here for the holidays?

HAROLD : A mustard tree Christmas tree?

MARILYN : Why not? They both represent faith.

HAROLD : But we'd have to come upstairs every time we wanted to see the treetop.

MARILYN : It's good exercise. And think of the money it'd save us. And every time we look at it, we'll be reminded of how just a little faith can have incredible results.

HAROLD: How 'bout some breakfast?

MARILYN: You expect me to sweep the floors and cook too?

HAROLD: All right, I'll help.

MARILYN (*surprised, glances heavenward*): He really is a God of miracles.

HAROLD (*as they exit*): And after we eat, we'll start decorating. Hmmm . . . mustard tree Christmas trees . . . now there's something I could sell on eBay!

Blackout

Mother

by Jim Custer and Bob Hoose

Scripture Reference: 2 Corinthians 4:4-6

Theme: Witnessing; How our faith is sometimes an offense to others.

Cast:
> JAN—Mid- to late 40s. Used to her mother's antics, but still affected by them. A sincere Christian who doesn't have all the answers.
> MOTHER—Sixty plus. Has had years of practice sharpening her skills in manipulation as well as her dry wit.

Setting: A living room, decorated in muted '60s earth tones. Pacing should be brisk.

Props:
> Cups
> Pack of cigarettes sitting on a table

Lighting: Basic wash

Running Time: 7 minutes

(Opens with JAN *sitting in family room of her parents' home. She is upset but working to control her emotions.* MOTHER *enters.)*

MOTHER: Here's your coffee, but it's hot. You'd better blow on it.

JAN *(shoots* MOTHER *a look, beat):* Mother, when will you ever stop smoking? I'm getting a buzz just sitting in here.

MOTHER: Don't you start on me. It's my only pleasure left in life. They've taken away all the rest. Besides, you know I never smoke in here . . . only in the kitchen.

JAN *(picks up coffee and blows on it):* Right, only in the kitchen. My mouth tastes like the bottom of an ashtray. I probably smell like one too.

MOTHER: Never used to bother you before. You never even noticed as I recall. But then, we don't see you much anymore. Things change, I suppose.

JAN: Yeah, well back then I was too young to know any better. Of course, one advantage was I never had to experiment with smoking. While the other kids were sneaking behind the public pool with their Marlboros, all I had to do was take a deep breath in my own living room.

MOTHER *(beat, while she looks at* JAN*):* I never smoked in the living room. But, just add one more brick to my load of rotten qualities. I drive my husband

41

to the grave with sin and now I'm a heartless mother who poisons her children . . . in the living room.

JAN (*drops head, exasperated*): Mom.

MOTHER: No, no. I know exactly how you feel. You made that very evident last night.

JAN: I . . . look, let's not do this. I don't need this now.

MOTHER (*a bit overdramatic*): Oh. Of course. You've had a great loss. I almost forgot. I guess I'll just put on my party dress and go dance in the streets. (*Gets up to take cup to kitchen*)

JAN: Moth . . . That's not what I meant. I meant, it's been difficult for everyone, that's all. I didn't want to fight . . . and I never said you were a bad mother. I'm just worried about you . . . the smoking, I mean. But . . . that's, oh, never mind. (MOTHER *sits back down. Pause*) Are you going to be all right?

MOTHER: What?

JAN: Will you be all right . . . alone, on your own?

MOTHER: I'm a big girl, Janny Marie.

JAN: I know. But this will be the first time you've been by yourself, in what . . . 40 some years?

MOTHER: Yes. But not for long. Old Mr. Morton, down the block, has already been giving me the eye. I think it's those Capri pants I bought last spring.

JAN (*exasperated*): Mom.

MOTHER: I'll be fine. Now, sit up straight, stop slouching. (JAN *straightens up automatically.* MOTHER *sips on coffee.*) Why did you do that last night, anyway? I was so embarrassed. I almost wished I was the one dying.

JAN (*taken back*): Huh?

MOTHER: He didn't hear you, you know. Everyone else in the room did, of course. But he didn't. I'm not sure he even knew if any of us were there.

JAN: I think he did. (*Pause*) I had to, Mom. I just wasn't sure he ever . . . I mean I had talked to him other times, but I wasn't sure. So I had to . . . no matter what.

MOTHER: Didn't you see how awkward you made everyone feel? Standing there preaching like Charlton Heston parting the Red Sea. I half expected your hair to turn white. (*Beat*) Your father was a good man. But, you . . . it was like you were waving a red flag and announcing that he was . . . (*Sighs heavily, dismissing it*) I don't understand you any longer.

JAN: No, you don't. And I'm not sure Dad did either. That's why I said what I . . .

42

OK, look . . . think of it like this . . . *(Beat)* If I were in a house on fire, what would you do?

MOTHER: Well, I'd roll you up in a rug or towels or something to put it out.

JAN *(beat):* No. I'm not on fire . . . the house is on fire.

MOTHER: This is a cigarette thing again, isn't it?

JAN: No. No. Go along with me on this, OK? I'm in a house that's on fire, but I don't see it. You do. What would you do?

MOTHER: I'd call the fire department.

JAN: Wait. No. This isn't that tough. I'm in the house, you're outdoors. OK?

MOTHER: I'd call from the neighbors.

JAN: But, I'm in the house. You gonna leave me in the house?

MOTHER: No. But when I ran out to the neighbors, you'd probably follow me out.

JAN: OK, OK, wait. I'm in the bathroom. I don't see you run out. I'm totally oblivious to the fire.

MOTHER: How would I know you're in there?

JAN *(getting frustrated):* I don't know. You see me. You peek in the window.

MOTHER: I wouldn't peek in the bathroom window. What if it were your Uncle Fred?

JAN: No. *(One more try)* OK. OK. Uncle Fred is in the bathroom. The house is on fire. Would you leave him in there? No. What would you do?

MOTHER: Run. Your Uncle Fred and fire do not mix in the bathroom.

JAN *(beat):* You're being deliberately obtuse, aren't you?

MOTHER: I'm not stupid, Janny. I know what you're trying to say. But, last night was such bad timing.

JAN: I didn't have any time. I've talked to Dad before, but I just wasn't sure. You may brush off faith in Christ as just silly religion, but . . . it's really all we have in the end.

MOTHER: Fine. Just, please don't embarrass me like that . . . especially in front of your Uncle Fred.

JAN *(makes a short, exasperated laugh/snortlike sound and shakes her head in resignation):* Mother . . . you drive me crazy.

MOTHER: Well, I may not have all of life's answers like you in your perfect religious world, but I'm quite content in my little smoky house . . . that's not on fire.

JAN (*smiles tiredly*): I never said anything about a perfect life. (*Laughs*) I'm forty plus years old. I watch my body swell up and break down in the mirror day by day. I have a healthy, maladjusted daughter who has driven me insane for the last seven or eight years, leaving the house for college this year. And for some stupid reason I already miss her. John is tied up in his job, but suddenly I'm without one. I don't know what to do anymore. I feel guilty for wanting a facelift or a butt tuck and angry because I need one. I've got changes and emotions rushing at me from all directions, and while I know that this is somehow in God's perfect plan for things, I don't understand it, or much of anything for that matter.

MOTHER (*pause*): Well . . . good. Want a cigarette?

JAN (*allowing herself to smirk at her mother's suggestion*): No. The one thing I do understand though . . . is that God is somehow in miraculous control of all this. I don't know what it all means, but I know that for some crazy reason He loves us and wants to help us make it through, right up to that last day. That's what I needed to tell Dad.

MOTHER (*long pause*): I suppose you did. (*Looking at each other.* MOTHER *reaches out and smooths* JAN's *hair as she used to do when she was a little girl.*) What was that little quote that your father always used to toss around?

JAN: Uh. You mean . . . "Love is worth nothing till it's given away"?

MOTHER: Well, I was thinking of "You can pick your nose, but you can't pick your relatives" . . . but yours will do. (JAN *laughs.*) Come on . . . I need a cigarette. (*They start to exit into kitchen.*) You can tell me some more cheery burning house stories.

Blackout

RURD4 Dehumanifier

by Jeff Smith

Scripture Reference: 1 Corinthians 1:18-21

Theme: The wisdom of man is foolishness to God.

Cast:
ANNOUNCER (M/F)—Nondescript
DR. HOFFENHEIMER (M, 50 plus)—Intellectual and highly academic. Play as a stuffy preacher or stiff seminary professor.
3 ACTORS (M/F adults)—Nondescript

Setting: A lecture or sermon setting.

Props:
Cellular phone or device that serves as a RURD4 Dehumanifier

Running Time: 3 minutes

(Stage as a commercial. ANNOUNCER can be an offstage voice or visible to the audience in a DSR position. Scene begins with DR. HOFFENHEIMER giving a lecture. ACTORS in "audience" seem bored or terribly confused. ANNOUNCER stands "outside" scene, looking in.)

ANNOUNCER: Dr. Hoffenheimer's sermon [lecture] on Harmatiology seems to have left his congregation clueless. One has to wonder who is missing the point. Let's listen in . . .

DR. HOFFENHEIMER: Even a perfunctory consideration of the prolegomena of dogmatic existentialism that drives cosmological implications of immutability inevitably engenders a dealing with timeless religio-moralistic doctrinarianisms . . .

ANNOUNCER: Now, watch what happens to our hapless audience whenever someone uses the new RURD4 Dehumanifier.

ACTOR 1: What is he talking about?

ACTOR 2: He said we need help.

ACTOR 3: You're kidding!

ACTOR 1: How did you know that?

ACTOR 2: Well, I just dialed up my RURD4 Dehumanifier and the voice-activated degarbler translated Dr. Hoffenheimer's babble into an easy-to-understand message that appears on the screen of my cell phone. (ACTORS *gather around cell phone with "oooohs" and "aahhhhs."*)

ANNOUNCER: It's as easy as making a call. Just dial 1-800-SPEAK-EZ and let there be LIGHT to that lost little mind of yours. Just think of it! No more baffling Christianese, over-the-top snubs, and heavy-handed putdowns by the holier-than-thou crowd. No more sidestepping questions from your kids after Sunday School because you don't know what they're talking about! With the Dehumanifier, you can be bored and still understand. And the Dehumanifier comes equipped with a games program for those really difficult-to-get-through messages. Just listen to these testimonials:

ACTOR 2 *(moving DSC):* I can go anywhere with my Dehumanifier and feel right at home. We attend a Baptist church on Sunday morning, a Pentecostal service on Sunday night, and a little Korean assembly for midweek services. I've never been more in touch with the Body of Christ.

ACTOR 3 *(moving DSC):* As a doctoral candidate studying Hermeneutical Eschatology, I began to find myself more and more isolated from mainstream Christianity. It was like I was losing touch with my humanity as I worked on my divinity . . . uh, divinity degree. But with the Dehumanifier, I can speak to the multitudes again.

ACTOR 1 *(moving DSC):* After using the Dehumanifier for just three weeks, I realized that I didn't agree with anything my pastor said and left my church to start my own Bible study.

ANNOUNCER *(if visible to audience, he or she joins ACTORS DSC):* Just think of it as Bible living for dummies. You'll be on the high road to godly living faster than you can say "sanctification."

ACTOR 3: What did he say?

ACTOR 2 *(referring to cell phone):* He said we got it!

ACTOR 1: Cool.

ANNOUNCER *(holding up a cell phone):* The Dehumanifier. It's slick, affordable, seeker sensitive, and speaker-friendly. The RURD4 Dehumanifier.

ALL ACTORS: Taking the mystery out of the mystery.

The End

Like a Thief

by Martha Bolton

Scripture References:

"For you know very well that the day of the Lord will come like a thief in the night" (1 Thessalonians 5:2).

"And if by grace, then it is no longer by works; if it were, grace would no longer be grace" (Romans 11:6).

"Remember, therefore, what you have received and heard; obey it, and repent. But if you do not wake up, I will come like a thief, and you will not know at what time I will come to you" (Revelation 3:3).

Themes: God's grace and forgiveness; Being ready

Description: Two men on two very different missions cross paths one night. One gets authenticity for his illustrated sermon, the other learns about grace.

Cast:

>Jess
>Sid
>Harry Walker
>Marcy Walker

Setting: The Walker Family home, living room

• a light switch (if not operational, then lighting should be controlled from elsewhere at the appropriate times)

• an intercom (doesn't need to be operational) should be on one side of the room

Props:

>Two flashlights
>Various pieces of living-room furniture
>A stereo
>VCR
>Television
>Trumpet
>Bible

Costumes: All black clothing

Running Time: 10 minutes

(Stage is dark. Jess enters SR, while Sid enters SL. They each are backing onto the stage. We see the lights of their flashlights dance around the stage. Jess and Sid continue backing onto the stage until they finally bump into each other in the darkness. They quickly turn around and shine their light in each other's face. They talk in a loud whisper.)

JESS: Who are you?

SID: Who are you?

JESS: I asked you first.

SID: All right, never mind . . . we'll do the job together; 70-30 split, no negotiating. Now, shhh! Follow me . . .

(JESS *follows closely behind* SID, *both shining lights around dark room.*)

JESS: You think they're here?

SID: Of course they're here. They're asleep. Now, keep your voice down! You're gonna wake 'em up.

JESS: OK. (*Beat, calls out loudly*) Hello? Can anybody hear me?

SID (*stops abruptly, turns around and shines flashlight directly into* JESS's *face):* What are you doing?!

JESS: Just giving them fair warning.

SID: Fair warning? What kind of a thief are you, anyway?

JESS: Well, you see, that's just it—I'm not a thief.

SID: You're not a thief?

JESS: No.

SID: Oh. (*Continues walking with* JESS *close behind, stops and thinks about that for a moment, quickly turns back and screams at* JESS *in a very loud whisper*) Then why are you here?!

JESS: Uh, yes, well, I can explain that. See, this is kind of a . . . well, it's an illustrated sermon.

SID: Oh. (*Continues a few more steps, stops, and turns around*) An illustrated what?

JESS: Sermon. See, I'm doing a little drama, showing how when Jesus returns, it's gonna be like a thief in the night.

SID: Drama? So you're an actor?

JESS: Yeah. How 'bout you? Why are you here?

SID: I'm robbing the place.

JESS: So you're for real?!

SID: Yeah, and you're really starting to annoy me.

JESS: I've never met a real robber before. (*Shines light in* SID's *face. They stare at each other.*)

SID: Boo!

(JESS *screams, drops flashlight.*)

JESS: What'd you do that for?! *(Picking up flashlight)*

SID: Just a little office humor. Look, just do your little industrial whatever. . .

JESS: Illustrated sermon.

SID: . . . but I'm warning ya, you botch this up for me and I could get ugly . . .

(JESS *shines light in* SID'S *face, stares at him, pondering comment.*)

SID: Say "too late" and you're a dead man.

JESS *(moving light from* SID'S *face)*: Don't worry. I'll stay out of your way.

SID: See that you do!

(SID *walks around room, shining light and gathering a few things. After several beats . . .*)

JESS: You know, ya gotta admit it's kinda neat.

SID: What?

JESS: That you're in my sermon and I'm in your robbery.

SID: Oh, yeah . . . I'm all choked up. Now, zip it before I . . .

JESS *(reaches for the switch and turns on the lights)*: There. That's better.

SID: What are you doing?! Are you crazy, man?!

JESS: Just trying to shine some light in the darkness.

SID: Why don't you just rent a neon sign while you're at it?! Let the whole world know we're here!

JESS *(singing)*: "This little light of mine."

SID *(turns off light)*: Sorry, pal, but I prefer to work in the dark.

JESS: You're just like the world. *(Turns on light)*

SID: Look, I know this isn't your line of work, but our union recommends that we, number one, don't call out to the owners of the house while we're robbing 'em, and number two, don't turn on all the lights! Now outta my way!

(SID *tries to turn out lights again, but* JESS *blocks his reach.*)

JESS *(sings)*: "Hide it under a bushel, no!"

(SID *waits a beat, then defiantly turns the lights off.* JESS *waits a beat and turns it back on. They alternate this for a few more times, then when the lights are on . . .*)

SID: You're a nut case!

JESS: Just trying to get my point across.

SID: All right. Forget it. Let's just hurry this up and get outta here.

JESS: Hey, look! An intercom! *(Walks over to intercom, turns it on, and talks.)* Everybody! Wake up! You're gonna miss it!

SID *(rushes over, turns it off):* Now, what at are you doing?!

JESS: They need to wake up. *(Turns it on again)*

SID: You are really hurting my reputation here, guy! *(Turns intercom off)*

JESS: Sorry, but I'm on a mission from God. *(Turns on intercom again and starts singing, Broadway-style "Get Happy!" composed by Harold Arlen)*

SID: You had to pick this house tonight, huh?

JESS: The script called for an ordinary house in a middle-class neighborhood.

SID: Look, why don't we compromise—you just do what you came here to do and I'll do what I came to do.

JESS: Fine.

SID: Fine!

JESS *(finds trumpet on floor, picks it up):* If this doesn't do it, nothing will! *(Plays a few notes of "Reveille")*

SID *(grabbing trumpet):* All right! That's it!

JESS: I have to know that I tried everything to wake them up. Otherwise, I'm gonna feel terrible when . . . *(Accidentally knocks over something)*

SID: You did that on purpose. (JESS *smiles.*) All right, listen . . . I don't know a lot about good drama, I'm no theater critic or anything, but I thought you said the point of your play thingy was to show how this . . . what's His name again . . .?

JESS: Jesus.

SID: . . . how this Jesus is going to return like "a thief in the night."

JESS: Right.

SID: Well, that is my line of work and, this case being the exception of course, most thieves don't give a warning.

JESS: Exactly. But that's actually when He returns for real. This is just a play, remember. And until then, I've gotta give 'em every warning I can. *(Goes to intercom, starts singing "I'll Fly Away")*

SID *(noticing Bible, picks it up):* Well, looky here.

JESS: What?

SID (reading from cover): Holy Bible.

JESS: So they've got a Bible. What does that prove?

SID: You're preachin' to the choir.

JESS: Just because there's a Bible in the house doesn't mean they've read it.

SID: Face it, you're wasting your time. And I am, too. Now, stand back. I've got a little more shopping to do. (Starts gathering up a few more things)

JESS: Fine, they have a Bible, but what if they don't think they measure up? What if they believe they have to be perfect to get to heaven? What if they don't understand about grace and forgiveness?

SID: So that's the point of your irritated sermon?

JESS: Illustrated. And yes, that's the whole point. God's grace and forgiveness is the whole point of everything! Nothing else counts if we get that wrong.

SID: You're making it sound like even a thief can go to heaven.

JESS: A thief went to heaven right alongside Jesus after He was crucified.

SID: No way.

JESS (indicating Bible): It's all right there in that Book. But sometimes we miss it. It's not about what you've done. It's about what He's done. It's not our goodness that makes us acceptable, it's His forgiveness.

SID (a pensive beat, then . . .): Look . . . this isn't really working. Whatd'ya say we blow this place?

JESS: But they're still sleeping.

SID: You gave them fair warning. Besides, if the family misses the thief, it makes your irrigated sermon thingy even more . . . how do they say it . . . (critic voice) gripping.

JESS: And you said you don't know drama.

(As they begin to exit SR . . .)

SID: You know, I'm not saying I'm thinking about changing professions or any-thing just yet, and I don't think I'm ready to get all, you know, religious and everything, but I might be interested in hearing a little more about this . . . what's His name again?

JESS: Jesus?

SID: Yeah. (Continuing a few more steps, SID stops, looking at all the things he has in his hands.) Wait . . . I don't really need all this stuff. (Puts down stolen items) . . . So, this Jesus really took a thief to heaven with Him, huh?

JESS: He really did.

SID: So, maybe there's hope for me after all?

JESS: Grace. That's all any of us have.

SID: Amazing. Pretty amazing.

(Turns out light and exits SR. Stage is empty for a few beats, then HARRY and MARCIE WALKER enter from SL. They turn on light and glance around room.)

HARRY: See, honey. There's nobody here.

MARCIE: But I know I heard something.

HARRY: You're worrying again for nothing. Now, come on, let's go back to bed.

MARCIE: But . . .

HARRY: Look, I'm a very light sleeper. Nothing's gonna take us by surprise. Now, come on. There's nothing to worry about. Just go back to sleep.

(MARCIE exits. HARRY starts to exit, but turns back one last time and looks around the room uneasily. He turns out light and exits.)

Blackout

With Friends like These . . .

by Chuck Neighbors

Scripture References: 1 Corinthians 13:1–13; Galatians 6:1–10

Themes: Depression; Compassion; Listening

Cast:

> JOHN—A busy, self-absorbed worker
> ED—A worker with a lot of troubles. Very depressed
> MARIE—A worker, the happy-go-lucky type. Full of advice, but very little substance
> DAVE—Another worker, an expert on one-upmanship

Props:

> Coffee pot and fixings
> Several cups
> Book
> Sack lunch
> Pamphlet

Setting: Coffee-break time in the lunchroom. There are a couple of tables with chairs and a coffee station off to one side. Ed is seated at one of the tables. He is depressed and looks it. John comes in and sits across from Ed.

Running Time: 3 minutes

JOHN: You look down.

ED: Do I? I guess I am—a bit.

JOHN: What's wrong?

ED: You really want to know?

JOHN: Sure.

ED: Well . . . where do I begin? My wife is sick, flu or something. It's been real tough to cover for her with the kids, work, meals, and all. I am behind on our bills and just received a notice from the insurance company—they have denied our claim on the auto accident last month. In the meantime, we've been renting a car while ours is in the shop. Now we'll have to pay for the rental out of our own pocket . . . I don't know where we are going to get the money. Our "sweet" little Andy is suspended from school for fighting and—

JOHN (*too much information*): Sounds tough! I'm sorry. (*Couldn't care less, checks watch)* Say, I'd like to hear more about it, but I'm running a little behind. Gotta get back to my office. *(Exits)*

ED: Oh, sure . . .

MARIE *(enters crossing toward coffee station, notices* ED, *walks over):* Ed, you still sitting here sulking?

ED: Marie, you don't understand—

MARIE: Cheer up! Things can't be that bad.

ED: But they are, you see—

MARIE: Come on! Snap out of it, Ed. Smile!

ED: Marie!

MARIE: Chin up! *(Goes to coffee station and prepares coffee, sits at other table and begins reading a book)*

ED *(mocking, but not loud enough for* MARIE *to hear):* "Cheer up!" "Snap out of it!" "Smile!" "Chin up!" Aw—shut up!

DAVE *(enters with sack lunch, approaches* ED): Hi, Ed. Mind if I join you?

ED: No, be my guest.

DAVE: Thanks. What's happening? *(Long look)* You look depressed. *(Starts eating)*

ED: Yeah, I am.

DAVE: What's wrong?

ED: You don't want to know.

DAVE: Sure I do. Try me!

ED: Well . . . *(Pause, not sure he wants to risk it, then goes ahead)* To begin with my wife, Emily, is down with the flu real bad—which makes it extra hard—

DAVE: Hey, couldn't be as bad as the case I had last year! Man, I had it so bad! Fever for a week, goin' at both ends. It was gross! The worst part was the rest of the family had it at the same time. Talk about inconvenient. Is that all, just a little flu?

ED: No, that is not all, Dave. I've got some financial problems that—

DAVE: Oh, man! You don't know what financial problems mean until you see our mortgage! We're in over our head, big time. And we bought a new car this year, don't forget. You should see—

ED: Excuse me, Dave, but I have to go. *(Gets up and goes to coffee station)*

MARIE *(checks her watch, gets up to leave, stopping by* ED *on the way):* Say Ed, why don't you read this pamphlet? *(Pulls it from purse)* It might help.

ED: What! *(Reads title of pamphlet)* "Change Your World with a Smile." Good grief! *(Rips it in half; throws in trash can and exits)*

MARIE *(crosses to* DAVE*):* What an attitude!

DAVE: Yeah. What's gotten into him?

MARIE: Oh he's got a bad case of the blahs. He just needs to snap out of it, that's all. I tried to tell him to cheer up!

DAVE: Yeah, he was telling me about it, but believe me his troubles are nothing compared to mine. But look at me, I don't mope around all day long.

MARIE: Some people just seem to thrive on attention. They seem to like throwing a pity party, I guess.

DAVE: Yeah, I know what you mean. I tried to help him, too, but he just wouldn't listen.

MARIE: I gave him some good advice, but he scoffed at it. If he would only listen to reason.

DAVE: I just don't understand some people.

MARIE: Me either. Well, break time is over. We better go! *(Exit)*

The End